ANGELS OVER THE ALTAR

Text · ALFRED FRANKENSTEIN   Photography · NORMAN CARLSON

ANGELS OVER THE ALTAR

Christian Folk Art in Hawaii and the South Seas

UNIVERSITY OF HAWAII PRESS · HONOLULU · 1961

TO OUR MOST PATIENT, LOYAL, AND INDULGENT CRITICS

Sylvia Frankenstein and Ina Carlson

PUBLICATION OF THIS BOOK WAS MADE POSSIBLE BY GENEROUS GRANTS FROM THE FOLLOWING, WHOSE INTEREST AND ASSISTANCE ARE GRATEFULLY ACKNOWLEDGED: MRS. HELEN DE Y. CAMERON, MR. HAROLD L. ZELLERBACH, THE JULIETTE M. ATHERTON TRUST, THE SAMUEL N. AND MARY CASTLE FOUNDATION, THE CHARLES M. AND ANNA C. COOKE TRUST, THE McINERNY FOUNDATION, THE ZELLERBACH FAMILY FUND, AND THE J. D. AND HANA ZELLERBACH FUND.

INTRODUCTION

This book has needed doing for a long time. The Painted Church at Honaunau is a major tourist attraction on the Island of Hawaii, but, aside from tourists and residents of the Islands, there are all too few who are aware of the fact that such a major monument of folk art exists. Even among the privileged who have seen the Honaunau church, the other structures of similar type on the island are little known. Here for the first time is a complete discussion of the group in its entirety.

The leading role in the story to follow was played by Father John, a devoted servant of the Lord, whose vocation had called him to a land in which the memory of other gods still remained bright. Father John's purpose was clear: the propagation of the faith and the continuing instruction of the faithful. Certainly the Hawaiian environment had little about it to remind Father John of his native Europe, and his work was restricted of necessity to the comparatively small number of souls his parish contained. His purpose, however, was no less compelling than that which gave rise, in another land and at another time—but for the same reasons—to one of man's most magnificent conceptions, the Gothic cathedral. The church at Honaunau may be tiny in terms of physical size compared with the prototypes which Father John remembered, but its conceptual scale looms large.

Father John was not a professionally trained artist in an academic sense, and, as Mr. Frankenstein points out, the church would never have existed if he had been.

Instead, he was a true folk artist, one of those creatively motivated individuals who create in order to fulfill a felt need, regardless of the magnitude of the undertaking and entirely without concern for what a more sophisticated point of view would regard as the essential degree of technical knowledge and facility required for its solution. The richness of the result, however, belies the poverty of the artist's technical training and qualifies the church for the appellation of a true cathedral of folk art.

Such dedication as that of Father John and of his follower, Father Evarist, inspired dedication in others, and it is Hawaii's good fortune that such an inspiration led so professionally equipped an historian and author as Alfred Frankenstein to delve deeply into the fascinating tale of the way in which these painter-priests worked. Mr. Frankenstein has delved deeply indeed, with a devotion very like that of the artists themselves, and his findings make fascinating reading as well as authoritative history. For many years the Honolulu Academy of Arts has hoped that the story of the Painted Churches might find an author, but we had scarcely dared hope that such a combination of professional ability and matching dedication could have been brought to its telling.

The role which Norman Carlson has played in this book is equally important. Mr. Carlson would call himself an amateur photographer, but he is an amateur only in the sense that he makes photographs for the love of it. From another point of view, one must recognize that his aesthetic and human sensibilities are so developed as to qualify him as a true professional. In fact, the book is very largely the result of years of painstaking and devoted work on his part, during which time he made literally hundreds of photographs of the churches under discussion, not only for his own pleasure but out of a sense of responsibility for preserving a detailed record of their existence as well. Since this fruitful collaboration began he has made countless more, again for love of the job. Mr. Carlson's part has been much more than that simply of recorder, however, for it was in fact he who introduced the churches other than that at Honaunau to Mr. Frankenstein and who, therefore, should in a very literal sense be regarded as the progenitor of the study.

The reader will also discover that Father John may well have been influenced, to whatever degree, by another artist's attempt, for different reasons, to create single-handedly a grandiose religious project in France. As Mr. Frankenstein points out, that work has been allowed to deteriorate over the years because of shortage of money and lack of interest. Hopefully, this publication may serve still another, but no less important, purpose than that of making these churches better known to a wider audience—the building up of a sufficiently active interest among those who do know and love them to guarantee that what is left of the Painted Churches of Hawaii may never meet a similar fate.

ROBERT P. GRIFFING, JR.

Director, Honolulu Academy of Arts

CONTENTS

Text   page 3

Notes   42

Plates   45

List of Plates   98

Acknowledgments   101

ANGELS OVER THE ALTAR

In the hillside hamlet of Honaunau, not far from the City of Refuge
National Historic Park on the Kona Coast of the Island of Hawaii, stands
a little church which is all but unique in the annals of American art. Its
official name is St. Benedict's, but it is known throughout the Hawaiian
Islands as the Painted Church. All the tour parties that traverse the Kona
road stop there, for the fervor, fantasy, and naïveté of the paintings inside
this little Gothic box cannot fail to exercise their charm even on the most
imperceptive. The bright colors of the paintings, softened and enriched
by time; their pictorial surprises, inventions, and reminiscences; the romantic atmosphere of the whole as a monument produced in isolation with the
simple wood and house paint that came to hand—all this is immensely
appealing, and the Painted Church provides a sure-fire attraction with
which to break the monotony of the lava flows and coffee trees wherein
that landscape abounds. The tour guides emphasize the curious aspects of
the building—its columns that flower into palm trees, its Biblical scenes
that improve on the Bible, its altar wall, which, with carefully illusionistic
perspective, transfers the soaring reaches of a Gothic cathedral from Europe
to Honaunau—but St. Benedict's is no mere eccentricity. It is, rather, a
little masterpiece of imaginative functionalism, of unity between struc-

ture, adornment, and architectural purpose. It is easy to understand why it is called the Painted Church, but that phrase lays far too much stress on the paint.

Literacy was not high among the natives of Hawaii when the shadowy figure known in the Islands as Father John arrived at Honaunau in 1899, and so he built a church wherein the teachings of Catholicism might be made manifest through the visual image. He had done this before—no one knows how many times before—in Tahiti and the Marquesas, where he had been stationed for ten years before his transfer to Hawaii. We have not been able to determine how many churches Father John built and painted in French Polynesia, or whether, as on Hawaii, his example led other Catholic missionaries there to erect and decorate equally interesting churches of their own. The evidence indicates, however, that the Painted Churches of Hawaii are not singular freaks but expressions of a hitherto unnoticed folk-art tradition of considerable breadth and extent.

Old record books preserved in Rome show that Father John's baptismal name was Joseph Velghe. He was born in Courtrai, Belgium, on July 14, 1857. Twenty-one years later, having completed his military service, he entered an academy which had only just been opened at Sarzeau, in Brittany, by the missionary order commonly known, at least in the islands of the Pacific, as the Fathers of the Sacred Hearts. In 1883 occurred an event which was ultimately to prove of first importance to the history of art in Hawaii: Joseph Velghe became a novice at Miranda de Ebro, in Spain, where the Fathers of the Sacred Hearts conducted an Apostolic School. He remained at Miranda for the better part of two years, after which he studied at the Sacred Hearts' Scholasticate in Louvain; and on June 29, 1888, he was ordained priest. At their ordination, priests of the Congregation of the Sacred Hearts exchange their baptismal names for those of saints. Joseph Velghe therefore became Father Jean Berchmans Velghe, after the sixteenth-century Belgian who had been canonized in the years of his (Velghe's) own entry into the priesthood.

Ever since 1825, missionary work in the South Seas on behalf of the Roman Catholic Church had been entrusted exclusively to the Fathers of the Sacred Hearts. An exceptionally large number of these missionaries, including the famous Father Damien of Molokai, were Belgians, and it is not surprising that Father Jean Berchmans Velghe was sent to the Marquesas within four months of his ordination.

In those days the center of the Catholic missionary effort in the Marquesas was at Hatiheu, on the Island of Nukahiva. There Father John arrived in December of 1888, having left Belgium on October 5 of that year.

According to Father Patrick O'Reilly, who has written much on the history of the Catholic missions in the South Seas, Father John very quickly won a reputation for being "an enthusiast, of vivid and sprightly character," who "painted murals in churches, conducted choirs, organized a brass band, and played in pantomimes"; and in that fashion he conducted himself for the next ten years.

In August of 1888, only a few weeks before Father John's arrival, Robert **II** Louis Stevenson, wandering the South Seas in search of health and adventure, had visited Hatiheu and there made observations that have great bearing on our story:

About midway of the beach no less than three churches stand grouped in a patch of bananas, intermingled with some pine-apples. Two are of wood: the original church, now in disuse; and a second that, for some mysterious reason, has never been used. The new church is of stone, with twin towers, walls flangeing into buttresses, and sculptured front. The design itself is good, simple, and shapely; but the character is all in the detail, where the architect has bloomed into the sculptor. It is impossible to tell in words of the angels (although they are more like winged archbishops) that stand guard upon the door, of the cherubs in the corners, of the scapegoat gargoyles, or the quaint and spirited relief, where Michael (the artist's patron) makes short work of a protesting Lucifer. We were never weary of viewing the imagery, so innocent, sometimes so funny, and yet in the best sense—in the sense of inventive gusto and expression—so artistic. I know not whether it was more strange to find a building of such merit in a corner of a barbarous isle, or to see a building so antique still bright with novelty. The architect, a French lay brother, still alive and well, and meditating fresh foundations, must have surely drawn his descent from a master-builder in the age of the cathedrals; and it was in looking on the church of Hatiheu that I seemed to perceive the secret charm of mediæval sculpture; that combination of the childish courage of the amateur, attempting all things, like the schoolboy on his slate, with the manly perseverance of the artist who does not know when he is conquered.

The architect and sculptor whose work Stevenson discusses here was Michel-Eutrope Blanc, who had been trained as a carpenter in his native France, had been sent to the Marquesas in 1866 to serve as builder for the missionaries, and, responding to the needs and opportunities of his new situation, had trained himself in all the arts of stone. Stevenson's remarks about him may very well constitute the first salute in history from the world of the intellectual to the world of the living primitive or folk artist; it antedates by twenty years Picasso's famous dinner for the Douanier 5

II. *Brother Michel Blanc*

Rousseau, and it contains in essence all the arguments on behalf of the naïve which were used by critics like Holger Cahill and Sidney Janis when, in the 1930s, they discovered the John Kanes and the Morris Hirshfields of the United States. Stevenson's appreciation of Brother Michel can be applied, with very little change, to Father John's work at Honaunau; it, too, combines "the childish courage of the amateur, attempting all things, like the schoolboy on his slate, with the manly perseverance of the artist who does not know when he is conquered."

Brother Michel would seem to have been the *chef d'école* among the Christian folk artists of the South Seas, and one can readily imagine Father John, under his influence, painting his first murals in one of those wooden churches on the beach at Hatiheu. Father John wrote much for Catholic missionary journals and illustrated his articles with drawings of his own, but nowhere does he say a word about painting churches and nowhere does he mention Brother Michel. No matter. Father John paid Brother Michel the highest tribute one artist can pay another: he painted his portrait, and that portrait is preserved today in the archives of the Sacred Hearts in Rome. It confirms Stevenson's description of the man:

6

A type of all that is most sound in France, with a broad, clever, honest, humorous countenance, an eye very large and bright, and a strong and healthy body inclining to obesity. [At this time Michel, who had been born in 1832, was 56 years old.] But that his blouse was black and his face shaven clean, you might pick such a man today, toiling cheerfully in his own patch of vines, from half a dozen provinces of France; and yet he always had for me a haunting resemblance to an old kind friend of my boyhood, whom I name in case any of my readers should share with me that memory—Dr. Paul, of the West Kirk.

Between his arrival in 1866 and his death in 1899, Brother Michel erected all manner of structures in the Marquesas, but he is especially well known for four of them. In chronological order, these are:

1873: A colossal statue of the Virgin carved into a pinnacle of natural rock above the harbor of Hatiheu.

1874–1879: The church at Hatiheu described by Stevenson.

1881: A church at Taaoa, Island of Hivaoe.

1883–1886: The church at Atuona, Island of Hivaoe, which Stevenson also visited.

Of these four works, all but the second are still in existence. The statue of the Virgin, which reminded Stevenson of "a poor lost doll, forgotten there by a giant child," is inaccessible to photography, however, and we are unable to provide a picture of it.

The church at Hatiheu was destroyed by a tidal wave in 1945. Three weeks after its dedication, on May 7, 1879, Father Géraud Chaulet described it in the following terms:

The church at Hatiheu is thirty meters long, nine wide, seven high to the edges of the roof....The walls are sustained by eight buttresses, four on each side; and eighteen Gothic columns hold up the vault. There is a beautiful gallery reached by two staircases placed in the towers that frame the façade. These hexagonal towers are lighted by six Gothic windows. The choir has a parquetry floor and is separated from the nave by a Gothic balustrade. In fact, the entire church is Gothic except for the main portal, which is Roman.

Every buttress is crowned with a cluster of coral. Each steeple is surmounted by an iron cross surrounded at its base with a half-dozen small pinnacles which look like so many sentinels. The summit of the gable of the façade is ornamented with a wooden cross. Below this cross is a representation of St. Michael overthrowing the devil, a scene which greatly impressed the natives....A little above the main door two angels offer crowns to those who enter the sacred precincts. On either side of the door two archangels guard the sanctity of the temple with flaming swords in their hands. The gallery is illuminated by a fine rose window of stained glass, and the main body of the church receives abundant light through its Gothic windows, also filled with stained glass.

The capital of each column is ornamented with acanthus leaves and various emblems; fifty-six rays, twenty-eight on each side, spread over the tympanum of the vault, which is also decorated with emblems of various kinds. Among the statues, one must single out those of the Sacred Heart, the Holy Virgin, Saint Joseph, Saint Peter, and Saint Paul.

No trace of the Hatiheu church remains today, but a small, faint photograph of its façade, taken in 1900, is preserved in the Roman archives. In it one may distinguish a number of the features described both by Stevenson and by Chaulet, notably the relief of St. Michael overthrowing the devil, which is all but identical in composition with the relief on the façade at Taaoa, but is lighter in implicit weight, more graceful and elongated.

Stevenson was eager to know if Brother Michel had followed any models in his architecture and sculpture, but the artist said he had none; he had worked entirely from imagination. Without questioning the truth of this statement, one may point out that Brother Michel belonged in an ancient and honorable tradition, that of French religious folk sculpture, best known through the calvaries of Brittany, hard by the ancient province of Poitou, where Michel Blanc was born. The curious deformation of the figure of the Christ child on the façade at Atuona reminds one startlingly of the Breton calvaries, and so do many other details in Brother Michel's sculpture, but, unlike the folk carvers of Brittany, he must have seen and admired some baroque sculpture, too; hence his sunbursts, the wayward, convoluted folds of his drapery, and the highly dramatic spread-eagle stance of his battling St. Michael. Somewhat baroque, too, is the choir of twelve delightful angels, like tousle-headed altar boys, which Michel placed above the altar at Atuona; he was responsible for the reredos in this church as well as for the building as a whole and its exterior adornment.

More direct parallels to Brother Michel's work may be discovered some day when French folk sculpture as a whole is carefully studied. So far, only the folk sculpture of Brittany has been thoroughly examined, and this for an interesting reason: Paul Gauguin represented two examples of it in his pictures, *The Yellow Christ* and *The Green Christ*, both painted in 1889. Gauguin opened the eyes of the world to Breton image-making, and he should have seen the irony involved in the missionaries' use of Christian folk sculpture in a closely related style as a weapon with which to overthrow Polynesian religions which possessed a highly developed sculpture of their own. Perhaps he actually did see this. Early in 1903, during the last months of his life, Gauguin produced a number of works wherein reminiscences of Breton folk art are mingled with Polynesian images, religious and otherwise. At that time he was living in Atuona, on land he had purchased from the Bishop of the Marquesas, and he had only to lift his eyes to see Michel Blanc's church in the middle distance. He did not raise his eyes in that direction very often, however. In his last years Gauguin rebelled violently against the missionaries, the church, and civil authority, and never left his house to paint or sketch. If he ever stopped to look at Brother Michel's sculpture, he left no record of that fact, and if Michel influenced the works of Gauguin wherein Christian and Polynesian imagery are mingled, that influence was exercised unconsciously, so far as we can tell.

Stone and stucco can resist the Marquesan climate; not so paint, and it **III** is not surprising that nothing by Father John remains in the Marquesas. Bishop Louis Tirilly, Vicar Apostolic to those islands, says he knows of only one church by Father John in the archipelago; it was at Hatiheu and it was wrecked in a storm in 1933 or thereabouts, but the murals it contained had disappeared long before that.

A tropical fever of some kind forced Father John to leave the Marquesas in 1899. He proceeded to Tahiti, where he spent six months and where, according to the records, he painted a church or two, of which no trace remains. He went to Hawaii more or less by accident. He had originally been scheduled to go to South America, but a yellow-fever epidemic blocked the sea lanes, and he eventually turned up in South Kona, where he had charge of the Catholic churches in five villages—Honaunau, Kealia, Hookena, Honokua, and Hoopuloa. He made his headquarters at Honaunau. His first entry in the baptismal book there is dated December 17, 1899, and his last July 26, 1904, soon after which he returned to Belgium.

Father John's principal artistic effort during his years in South Kona was the present church of St. Benedict at Honaunau, which he designed, built, and painted, and which was consecrated in 1902. The original church of St. Benedict was on the shore at Honaunau, very close to the City of Refuge; it had been built there in the 1870s, and its site seems to have been chosen because at that time the Hawaiians still regarded the City of Refuge as a holy place. What motivated Father John in building a new church farther up the hill, we do not know; all we know is that he did so. In all probability he also painted the altar and interior decorations in the church of Maria Lanakila at Kealia. This building was toppled by an earthquake in 1950. It is now a ruin, but one of great interest, and we shall return to it later. The Catholic churches that existed in Hookena, Honokua, and Hoopuloa in Father John's time have long since disappeared completely, and no one today knows anything about them.

9

III. *Michel Blanc: Church at Taaoa, Hivaoe, Marquesas*

IV. *Michel Blanc: Relief on the façade of the Church at Taaoa, Hivaoe, Marquesas*

V. *Michel Blanc: Relief on the façade of the Church at Atuona, Hivaoe, Marquesas*

VI. *Michel Blanc: Church at Atuona, Hivaoe, Marquesas*

As we have seen, Father John went back to Europe in 1904. He was at the scholasticate in his birthplace, Courtrai, for two years, then lived for short periods in the monasteries of the Sacred Hearts, residing in a number of their establishments in the Low Countries. In 1935 he was confined in a Sanitarium at Lierre, Belgium, and there he died, on January 20, 1939.

Throughout his last years he continued to paint, and he achieved some celebrity among his fellow priests for his work as an artist. At least a few of his works are still preserved in Europe; the church of St. Anthony in Louvain is adorned with his "Seven Sorrows of Mary," copied from the like-named series of pictures by the once-famous Belgian painter, Joseph Janssens, which is, or was, in the Cathedral of Antwerp. While teaching at the Sacred Hearts' Apostolic School at Aarschot, Belgium, in 1923 or 1924, he met the young student, Matthias Gielen, who was to become Father Evarist of Hawaii, and briefly gave him instruction in drawing and painting, which was later to bear fruit in the churches at Mountain View and Kalapana to which we shall eventually come.

The entry on Father John in the annals of the Congregation of the Sacred Hearts at Rome concludes as follows:

He gladly gave all the service which his poor health permitted him to give, always remaining faithful to the art of painting, in which he might have excelled if he had had proper training. In our Mother House we have his portrait of the Very Reverend Flavien Prat, which exhibits his special manner: he was given to exaggerating the importance and the number of decorative details.

He held the brush almost to the end of his life, until the day when his poor eyes refused their service. When he realized that, even with the strongest glasses, he could no longer command the brush as he wished, he understood that God demanded of him a huge sacrifice which he dreaded.

His was a faithful soul capable of responding to the invitations of his divine crucified Master. His last three years were particularly miserable because of the special care which had to be taken of him.

IV The Roman annalist is entitled to his opinion; nevertheless, we may rejoice that Father John did not have academic training, and if he exaggerated detail in his later paintings, he did not do so at Honaunau. On the contrary, nothing at St. Benedict's Church is in the slightest degree disproportionate, and everything in it works. Its logical and harmonious ordering of shapes, colors, and relationships has been somewhat disturbed by alteration at its west end—the choir gallery and the area below it are clearly not as they were in Father John's time, and there is evidence to suggest that the space

below the choir gallery was originally partitioned off to form a vestibule—

VII. *Michel Blanc: Angels over the Altar, Church at Atuona*

but very little has been changed in the main body of the church, and it is with this alone that we shall be concerned.

The main body of the church is an oblong space divided into a nave and two side aisles. A long, high vault, shaped in cross section like a pointed arch, covers and defines the nave and is supported on each side by three columns. The two side aisles have comparatively low, flat ceilings. In each side wall, up to the edge of the choir gallery, where the partition probably stood, are three windows, each of them likewise in the shape of a pointed arch, and between them are panels painted at eye level with pictures of religious import. Above each of the pictures is a painted Gothic lunette. On the wall behind the altar are three painted views of a Gothic church. The large one in the middle continues the line of the vaulted nave into deep space, while the two smaller ones seem to branch off from the side aisles.

This, then, is the plan for the main body of St. Benedict's Church at Honaunau: three windows, three painted panels, and three columns on each side; three aisles, and three more painted pictures on the altar wall. It is like the threefold *Kyrie eleison*, threefold *Christe eleison*, and threefold *Kyrie eleison* with which the Ordinary of the Mass begins. However limited language may be in explaining the mysteries of the Church, the doctrine of the Trinity was clear enough in this architectural setting.

To build a vaulted Gothic nave inside a little gable-roofed box was a daring idea which would never have occurred to a trained architect, nor is a trained architect likely to have conceived Father John's solution to the problem of the apse and transepts which the existence of the nave immediately posed. To build these appendages was, clearly, outside the range of possibility at that place and time; Father John therefore painted them on the wall behind the altar, joining them, in illusionistically rendered perspective, to the "real" space; and he did so with such success that, in photographs at least, it is impossible to tell where the "real" vault ends and the illusion begins. Illusionistic perspective is used, however, primarily as a means of dramatizing light. The painter has been very specific about his richly ribbed vaulting, his fluted piers, his arched colonnades, and so on, but his drawing becomes less and less particularized as it ascends toward the illumination at its highest and farthest point. This light, rendered all the more radiant through its contrast with the dark, heavy, shadowed mass of the ribbed vaulting immediately before it, is the focal point for the architectural and pictorial design of the entire church. It carries the eye and the spirit upward toward infinity, as it does in the famous building which served Father John as a model.

For here, on the altar wall of the little wooden church at Honaunau, we gaze into the celebrated *cimborio*, or light-dome (what in architectural parlance is called a lantern) of the Cathedral of Burgos, in Spain. Until now it has been assumed that in painting the Gothic reaches on his altar wall Father John had drawn upon memories of some church in Belgium, or had simply invented a Gothic church, but this is not the case. The octagonal *cimborio* of Burgos, with its unique, unmistakable pendentives adorned with fan-shaped ribbing, is here reproduced in detail, as well as the fluted piers which support that dome, their crown-like capitals and their sculpture in niches, and the colonnaded arches that pierce the walls below the stained-glass windows nearby. This is the legacy of Father John's two years at Miranda de Ebro, some thirty-five miles from Burgos. No doubt he had sketched the cathedral during his novitiate, and one wonders how many representations of it are or were to be found in remote valleys of the Marquesas and Tahiti as well as at Honaunau.

On the wall immediately behind and above the altar, framed by the Gothic vault, Father John shows us the *cimborio* of Burgos Cathedral and the apse directly behind it. On the same wall, to the left and right of this large central panel and framed by the flat-ceilinged side aisles, we look through the *cimborio* into the transepts of the cathedral, each with a rose window at its end and a pair of arched colonnades immediately beneath this. The painted transepts turn the corner and are continued for a little space on the side walls; here, on the right-hand side, we may also see the unsupported circular staircase which is one of the most celebrated architectural features of Burgos. The right transept at Honaunau is disfigured by a blank door leading into the sacristy. Father Evarist believes that the representation of the transept covered this door as well as the wall space to the right of it in Father John's time.

In viewing these painted transepts we are, of course, supposed to be looking into the *cimborio* at right angles to the view thereof provided above the altar, but there is no way in which a ninety-degree shift of view can be indicated on a flat surface. Father John therefore renders the transepts with as much shift as he can summon; they move outward and break the confinement of the side walls like the arms of a Y, but we are to "read" them as if they were the arms of a T. No trained painter would have had the courage to invent such a device, nor would a trained artist have had the inventiveness to attempt Father John's solution to the difficulty that arose in the space directly behind the altar where the transepts, moving outward to each side, impinge upon the apse, which is here seen straight on. For these three perspective systems to flow together would have created the utmost confusion and ruined the effect. Father John therefore painted noth- 15 ing at all directly behind the altar, and that space is now covered with a mat. He separated apse and transepts completely. In the time-honored tradition of all Western folk painters, he substituted ambiguity for inconsistency and so saved the day.

The painted apse and transepts are markedly more vivacious, lighter, and sketchier in drawing than the panels of religious illustration on the side walls, and they are also freer and more spontaneous in their paint surfaces. Father John was a naïve artist, but he knew that a painting to be seen at a distance required different treatment from one to be seen close, and his representation of Burgos Cathedral carries more convincingly across the space of the sanctuary than if it had been done with the strongly linear and volumetric modeling employed, say, in his picture of Belshazzar's Feast. Observe well, also, that the colors employed in the painting of the cathedral—the rose and blue and reddish brown—harmonize perfectly with the colors employed in the sky and with those used in the palm fronds painted on the greater part of the vault immediately before it.

V The idea of painting the interior of a Gothic cathedral on the altar wall of his church was, in all probability, suggested to Father John by the very similar and, in its time, very celebrated painting by Louis Daguerre in the small parish church at Bry-sur-Marne, near Paris. Daguerre is remembered today for his contribution to the art and science of photography, but, as the Gernsheims remind us, he began his career as a painter of easel pictures, theatrical scenery, and dioramas; these last were enormous paintings on translucent linen which were exhibited in specially constructed buildings with special effects of light. In 1840 Daguerre bought a small property in the village on the Marne and

Wishing to create at Bry a permanent reminder of his residence there, Daguerre conceived the idea of decorating the church with a perspective painting behind the High Altar....For six months he worked with unabated energy on this last work, which was to be less ephemeral than his dioramas. Representing the interior of a fine Gothic cathedral with stained-glass windows, tombs of knights, and their banners hanging above, the painting included all the favorite effects which had delighted Parisian audiences. Light entering the nave from the right strikes the pillars, on some of which hang paintings of Biblical subjects so perfectly represented that it seems one could unhook them. A beam of light strikes some cobwebs apparently spun only that morning. One of the candles has just gone out, and the still smoking wick sends smoke into the air. Bouquets of flowers are painted so realistically that you want to touch them. But the most important *trompe-l'oeil* effect only became apparent when the 13 ft. x 19 ft. 6 in. painting was unveiled on 19 June 1842. On entering the

16

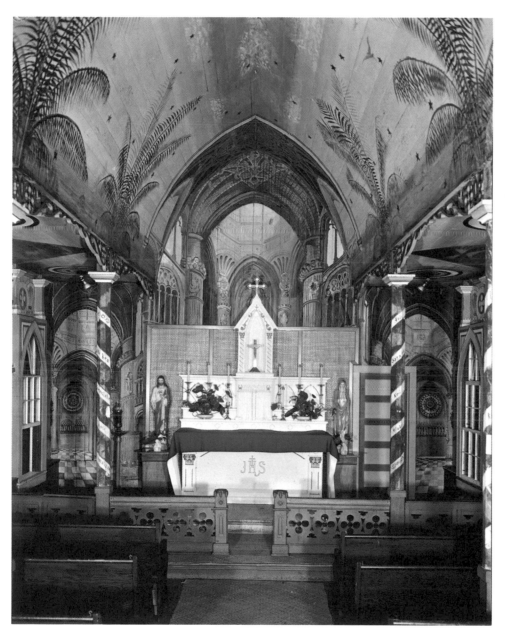

VIII. *Honaunau: General view of the interior*

little church the community of Bry was transfixed with astonishment: Daguerre's magic art had transformed the simple little church into a grand cathedral twice its real length. Up to World War I the painting was classified as a national monument, but shortage of money and lack of interest have allowed it to deteriorate since.

Gothic architecture, intact or, better still, in ruins, was a favorite theme with Daguerre, as it was with all the artists, poets, and opera librettists of his time. His most famous easel picture, painted in 1824, represents the ruins of Holyrood Chapel, and at least a third of Daguerre's known paintings, drawings, and dioramas, as listed by the Gernsheims, deal with similar themes. But between Daguerre, the cultivated romantic, and Father John, the folk painter, there lies a distinction of no mean interest or significance.

Romanticism invested the Gothic with its own macabre dreams and its peculiar sense of the insecurity of life. All the *trompe-l'oeil* painting of the romantic period rings changes on one idea, that man cannot distinguish illusion from reality; the diorama expressed this idea with the spectacular, Mephistophelean wizardry to which romanticism was so partial. There is even a whiff of brimstone about the painting at Bry; among other things, this work reverses the relationship of church and altar in a most extraordinary and totally uncanonical way.

For Daguerre's painted wall at Bry does not represent a Gothic apse but the entire length of a Gothic nave. The beholder is presumed to be standing in a sanctuary under a lantern like the *cimborio* of Burgos, looking toward the main portal of the church in the far distance; extra-large arches on either side clearly indicate where the transepts join on. The implication of Daguerre's arrangement is that the real church is merely the apse of the painted church, but then, inevitably, the real altar stands with its back to the nave, as no proper altar should. In other words, Daguerre, the romantic, emphasizes illusion at the expense of reality, but as soon as one asks the naïve question, "Where is the real altar in relation to the painted church?" his illusion collapses completely.

Father John doubtless passed through Paris several times during his student days at Sarzeau and Miranda in the '70s and '80s, when the reputation of Daguerre's painting was at its height. The probability of his having been inspired by Daguerre's example is very strong, but he asked the naïve question. Furthermore, he was no entrepreneur of the spectacular. He was content to paint the relatively modest space of a Gothic apse, and, of course, he preserved the proper relationship of church and altar. He approached the theme entirely on the side of reality as he understood reality; at Honaunau, romantic *trompe l'oeil* is redeemed from its Mephistophelean overtones. Observe also that Father John did not invent a church, as Daguerre did, but transported the Cathedral of Burgos to his lava-crusted hillside in the minute Hawaiian village of Honaunau on the Kona Coast.

The vault over the nave at Honaunau is finely proportioned, and, as is observed above, was no mean architectural feat for its place and time. Each of its supporting columns is octagonal but stands on a square pedestal. The octagonal shafts are painted red, with splotches of green and yellow to suggest the veining of marble. Each is encircled five times with a painted white ribbon bearing, on the side facing the congregation, one of the mottoes of St. Benedict's medal in Hawaiian.

Each column bears a square capital made of prefabricated moulding and painted white, ochre, yellow, blue, and green. Between these capitals, fringing the lower edges of the vault throughout their length, are long pieces of jigsaw scrollwork painted green and black on their sides and yellow on their edges. The columns thrust up through their capitals in the form of square posts and burst into palm trees, their stems painted on the posts, their gracefully arching branches making symmetrical patterns on the vault. These lofty aerial fronds are beautifully and powerfully designed. They spring from the capitals like Gothic ribbing; they also remind one of the palm-leaf designs that adorn the interiors of some ancient mosques.

There are six palm trees on the vault at Honaunau, and in each of them the fronds pointing away from the altar bear dead leaves, painted brown and yellow, while the leaves on the side toward the altar are almost entirely fresh and green. The symbolism requires no comment, but this arrangement was also dictated in part by Father John's instinct for color. Observe that on each tree a few of the leaves on the altar side are slightly edged with brown—just enough to hold the entire color composition together and prevent its splitting in two.

Below the palm trees the vault is painted in an ascending pattern of light. Along its lowest course is a deep blue suggesting an indistinct sea horizon. This mounts through red and yellow, with sketchy dark clouds like distant, low-lying islands, to a bright sky-blue with white clouds; there are also a few flying birds here and there. The whole is a very precise representation of sunset as one sees it from the steps of the church. But naïve stylization counters realism here in the stars cut out of sheet metal and tacked on all over the vault.

VII Each of the six panels on the side walls between the windows is divided into two unequal spaces by a horizontal beam decorated with white scroll-work. The upper and smaller space takes the form of a lunette filled with Gothic tracery imitated from that of Burgos Cathedral. Each lower space contains a religious picture roughly eighty inches wide and fifty-two inches high. Justly or unjustly, these pictures are primarily responsible for such celebrity as the church has enjoyed. They are the subject of almost all the comment on St. Benedict's which has appeared up to the present, and some of them have been widely reproduced in Hawaiian publications. We must therefore study them carefully, both individually and as a group.

The first thing to be said about them as a group is that Father John made no effort to maintain consistency of scale among them; the spectator is now close to and now far away from the represented scenes. Pursuing this observation further, one perceives another, far stranger, more baffling, and more entertaining inconsistency among the six pictures. They remind one a little of the paintings that used to hang in the Thomas Waterman Wood Museum at Montpelier, Vermont—those copies of Rubens, Titian, Turner, and others which faithfully imitate the stylistic traits of the originals but are nevertheless inevitably and eerily in the single style of the copyist, Thomas Waterman Wood.

Father John's six pictures on the side walls at Honaunau provide a somewhat similar anthology of styles unified by a single style. Unlike Wood, however, Father John was not motivated by a desire to further the artistic education of his beholders with a gallery of *ersatz* old masters, and he left no record of his sources.

Perhaps some, perhaps most of his pictures at Honaunau are entirely his own, but we have found the specific source for one of them and for part of another, and this, viewed in conjunction with Father John's variety of approaches, leads one to suspect that all his pictures are indebted to pre-existing works of art. This, however, is merely suspicion. Folk artists copy and invent indiscriminately, and in art history, as in Anglo-Saxon law, a man is innocent until proven guilty, if "guilty" is the word to be used in this context. Folk artists eagerly accept the work of established masters as models for their own compositions. It is a sign of humility in Edward Hicks, the Quaker preacher and painter, that he appropriated ideas left and right from Benjamin West, John Trumbull, and the prints of Currier and Ives, and a similar humility is to be assumed in the case of Father John, but his borrowings are much more difficult to track down than those of Hicks.

An elaborate research project carried on for years might, perhaps, solve the problem of these six paintings, but such a project would not be worth while. We have done such research as seemed warranted, going through the standard books on Christian iconography, consulting art historians well acquainted with that field, and turning over several thousand photographs and other reproductions in the archives of the Frick Reference Library and the New York Public Library. What we have found is meager, but all of our evidence points in one direction.

Father John and Father Evarist, who is still very much alive and who readily gave us his sources, were particularly impressed with European academic painters of the late nineteenth century who were famous men in their own time, held all the professorships, won all the medals, and were awarded all the mural commissions, but who in terms of today's "art world" are more thoroughly dead and buried than the least apprentice in the most insignificant of Renaissance workshops. So far as modern art history is concerned, these painters have never existed, and consequently they are represented in the libraries organized to serve contemporary art history only in the most fragmentary way, and then by accident. But the "art world" is not the whole world, and there exist vast strata of art which art history totally ignores, and here the nineteenth century academicians maintain a subterranean existence. Their works are reproduced on religious calendars, pamphlets, and other fugitive publications which are distributed in millions of copies each year. Their very commonness prevents one's attempting to find them; there are some things for which life is too short.

Be that as it may, artists like Bernhard Plockhorst and Joseph Janssens, who we know were copied by Father John and Father Evarist, were strongly archaistic in style; they, and many other academic religious painters active in the latter part of the nineteenth century, represent the final, forgotten phase of the archaism launched earlier in the century by the Nazarenes of Germany and the Pre-Raphaelites of England. Now, when a folk painter like Father John or Father Evarist follows an archaistic model, the result looks as if he had gone directly to the source. The walls at Honaunau and Kalapana are full of pictures seemingly imitated from primitive and early Renaissance masters, but one looks in vain for their prototypes in the periods which have apparently been drawn upon. Primitive and early Renaissance art has been filtered through nineteenth-century academic adaptations which, in most instances, have been lost beyond recovery. Here, then, is an extremely curious layering, twisting, thrust and counterthrust of period styles, and the effort to disentangle them leads one into mystery upon mystery. But one thing is sure: the folk painters validate the archaistic tendencies of their models. With them, the archaic is not a mannerism. Primitives themselves, they understand the primitive with a far surer instinct   21 than the academicians through whom their knowledge of primitive art was apparently derived.

With these general considerations in mind, let us go about the walls at Honaunau, taking as our guide the series of paper labels tacked above each picture and providing a title for each in a marvelously frilly, old-fashioned penmanship like that which Saul Steinberg uses in his cartoons.

VIII The first picture on the left near the door is called "The Handwriting on the Wall." Thanks to its sumptuous, warm, Venetian colors, its spaciousness, and its dramatic handling of numerous figures, this painting is a primitive Veronese. Its highest point of light is, of course, the handwriting on the wall, to which the upright Daniel points; it bursts forth in a kind of gloriole, in the Hawaiian language—*Ua emi loa oe / Ua pau kou aupuni / Make no ka pono.* (Literally, "You are found wanting / Your kingdom ceases / Should die.") The bearded, burly king, whose head is so nicely silhouetted against the large gray oval of a long-handled fan held by an attendant, receives this news with a troubled expression and a dramatic downward gesture of his left arm, extended and reinforced by the reclining body of his queen, who turns her face away and clasps Belshazzar's right hand. The group of three figures at the lower right, who perceive the handwriting on the wall with gestures of despair, stops and builds up a countermovement to the diagonal of the royal personages. In the distance, the people of Belshazzar's court gaze at the handwriting with gestures which grow more and more extreme as they recede. In the far distance we see wildly flailing arms under a balcony; here Father John has thinned out his color in an attempt at atmospheric perspective which makes these figures look like some strangely eruptive sculpture in relief. One of the picture's most interesting stylistic peculiarities is that although several of its figures are presented in profile, their eyes are drawn as if seen from the front; here Father John looks back to ancient Egypt or forward to Picasso, as you choose. This may be observed in the figure of Daniel and even more clearly in the figure below him with hands clasped on the table top. We shall have occasion to return to this trait of Father John's later on in an important place.

The "Handwriting on the Wall" relies very heavily upon line for its modeling and its delineation of forms; the next picture, "The Temptation of Jesus," makes very little use of line and relies primarily upon color and tone. The long-haired, rather sweet figure of the beardless Christ is of the nineteenth century, and so is the perspective drawing of the landscape, with its mountains, waterfall, and river valley receding into deep space in mild,

IX. *Honaunau: The Handwriting on the Wall*

pastel-like hues, but the symbolic disproportion between the figure of Jesus and the mountain on which he stands is medieval, and medieval in a manner that would not be attempted by any nineteenth-century academician, no matter how archaistic. Equally of the Middle Ages is the distant town, with its turrets and towers drawn so very much smaller than the surrounding trees, but the most strikingly medieval thing of all is the naked, bat-winged devil whom Christ has cast down and who falls through the air along with the scepter, crown, and bags of money he has offered. This reptilian fiend is a Gothic grotesque, and his kind scarcely outlasted the Gothic age, at least in representations of this subject; in Renaissance and more modern "Temptations," the devil usually appears in disguise as a scholar, a rich man, or a monk. However deeply Father John may have been impressed with the academic celebrities of his own time, he here returns to traditions more ancient and honorable than theirs.

The third picture on this wall is "The Appearance of the Cross to St. Francis." The kneeling figure of the saint and the apparition of Christ on the Cross, surrounded by wings and flames and glowing all the more hotly for the cold dark of their surroundings, have a decidedly Giottesque appearance, and the setting—rocks and a distant town—has innumerable parallels in the works of medieval and Renaissance artists. But the particular setting chosen by Father John is beyond comprehension and would be beyond belief if it could not be conclusively proved. For Father John has represented   23

St. Francis receiving the stigmata on the famous tunneled road known as the Axenstrasse, near Lucerne. It is identified as such by Sydney Clark, the professional globetrotter, in his book, *All the Best in Hawaii*. In verifying Clark's assertion, we discovered the specific photograph of the Axenstrasse which Father John employed. It is reproduced in Oscar Kuhns's *Switzerland*, published in 1910, but it must have been in existence at least six years before Kuhns's book was published. Father John copied it line for line, detail for detail, omitting only the electric wire and its supporting bracket which show in the original. In the photograph, a Swiss mountaineer peers out over the parapet beneath the second rough-hewn arch. Father John changes this to a priest, who gazes serenely over the lake totally unmindful of the miracle taking place behind his back. Why Father John should have placed St. Francis receiving the stigmata on the Axenstrasse we do not know; perhaps it was just a cave to him, and, as we have observed, the subject belongs traditionally in or near a cave; perhaps, also, there was some symbolism or association of ideas in his mind to which we do not have the key.

Half a century of tropical noonday sun has beaten on the right-hand or south wall of the church, and as a result the pictures here are in worse condition than those elsewhere. On the whole, time has dealt nobly with Father John's colors and has given them dignity and luster, but on the south wall heat has cracked the paint and brought pitch from the boards to loosen and puddle it. The picture called "Hell" at the west end is a ruin; still and all, it is obviously more impressive in that state than it ever could have been when fresh. A great, lusty, bull-horned Satan, with greenish-blue skin, sparks emanating from his now-ruined eyes, and his red tongue protruding, throws back his head and gazes defiantly at heaven as he stretches his huge arms in triumph over his victims, a weeping, reviling, naked, and tormented crew worthy of Masaccio. Flames envelop the human figures and monstrous, half-legible serpents and octopi slither about, giving the entire composition an effect of bloody, visceral horror which Pavel Tchelichew would have envied. According to Father Evarist, Father John painted representatives of all the races of mankind in hell. The majority of those now visible are *haoles*, but at the lower left is a Chinese with a pigtail and at the far right is a crowned Hawaiian queen—probably Kaahumanu, who persecuted the Catholics when they first came to the Islands. In the best surrealist tradition, new faces appear in the bubbling wreck of this picture whenever one returns to it. Its dripping mixture of crystallized pitch and crackled paint gives it a peculiarly evil scintillation; many an abstract expressionist would give his little finger to create a surface like that which Father John and the sun of Hawaii have brought to being here.

24

The second painting on the right-hand wall bears the title "Symbolic Picture=Symbolic of a good Death / Rays of Hope shining in the Dark Cell." A woman in a white robe trimmed with blue lies on a slab, with a cross on her chest and a delicately indicated halo about her head. Flowers and a ewer fill the lower right corner. At the upper left are heavy geometric forms, obviously intended to suggest the interior of a cell, and rays of light streaming from under a barred window. If the walls of the cell proceeded all across the painting at the angle on which they have been drawn, they would cut the human figure in two, and Father John therefore stops them in mid-course; behind the greater part of the woman's figure is an expanse of flat darkness in which she seems almost to float. The woman's long black hair, her bulbous, closed eyes and small mouth hold one's attention by virtue of their serenity, and the picture's ambiguous use of space adds a telling touch of the mysterious.

The last of the pictures on the right-hand wall bears the label "Cain and Abel (and Eve trying to revive him)." In the few lines he devotes to the Painted Church, Sydney Clark pokes fun at Father John for improving on Scripture here, but the improvement is not the work of Father John but of the unknown person who wrote the labels. Eve is not trying to revive Abel; she is merely finding his body. The painting is a copy of "Eve Finding the Body of Abel" by Karl Gebhardt (1860-1917), who in his time was a leading figure of the Munich school. He exhibited frequently in Munich and Berlin from 1883 until his death, stressing religious subject matter in the early part of his career. We do not know the date of "Eve Finding the Body of Abel," but it is at least conceivable that Father John became acquainted with it, in the original or in reproduction, before he went to the South Seas. The picture must have had more than ordinary acclaim, since it is one of the three works of Gebhardt specifically mentioned in the article on this artist in Thieme and Becker's *Allgemeines Lexikon der Bildenden Künstler.* In 1908, Charles F. Horne and Julius Bewer reproduced it in their huge book, *The Bible and Its Story Taught by One Thousand Picture Lessons.* Copies of the wood engraving published by Horne and Bewer ultimately found their way into the archives of the Frick Art Reference Library and the New York Public Library, where we discovered them in the course of our research. The painting by Bernhard Plockhorst copied by Father Evarist at Kalapana is also to be found in Horne and Bewer, but none of the other pictures with which we are concerned.

Father John had access to a better copy of Gebhardt's painting than the one in *The Bible and Its Story.* On comparing the two versions one may see that the engraving has been cropped at the bottom, so that Abel's right arm 25 is cut off at the elbow; in the Honaunau version, Abel's entire right arm droops in death over a rock, and all the figures are properly framed in the pictorial space. If the wood engraving can be believed, Father John has given these figures much greater tension, anguish, and violence than they had in the original; no wonder the writer of the labels thought Eve was trying to revive her younger son! Father John has simplified Gebhardt's rocky background. How the two versions compare in color, we cannot say. Father John's color is very dark, stormy, and cold. The sinister coast and lowering, evil birds at the left properly compliment the picture's major theme.

The lunettes above the six pictures on the side walls at Honaunau are, with one exception, identical. Each has a green background against which stand seven little Gothic pinnacles painted in grayish-blue outlined with black, and above them is a pattern of Gothic tracery in yellow; the upper corners of each of these panels are filled with bright red spandrels. According to Father Eugene Oehmen, who succeeded Father John as priest of St. Benedict's, the artist had originally intended to paint figures of saints in the niche-like spaces between the pinnacles, but he was recalled to Belgium before this part of the work could be completed. He did paint saints, however, in the lunette above the picture of St. Francis. On the left are Paul and Peter, on the right Joseph and John the Baptist. In the center, painted over the middle pinnacle, is a group of three figures. Christ, displaying the Sacred Hearts, blesses two other figures: Jesus, bearing his cross, clasping the hand of a woman in a red robe who faces him. Father Francis Kelliher, until recently priest of St. Benedict's, suggests that the female figure stands for Hawaii and that the whole symbolizes the preaching of the Gospel in the Islands. Lithographed Stations of the Cross have been placed over all six lunettes, so that they are difficult to see today.

For the rest, a few matters of adornment must be accounted for. Spandrels, painted with rectilinear patterns of light blue and white, enliven the tops of the window cases. Above each window is a small panel containing a cruciform rosette supported on each side by a twisted, five-fingered shape derived from the fan-ribbed pendentives supporting the *cimborio* of Burgos, and this form is echoed throughout the building. The panels above the windows are framed with small square columns painted the same light blue as the window-spandrels, but with bases and capitals of ochre and white.

The ceilings over the side aisles bear alternating triangles of dark blue and white, each shading into dark gray at its apex. The blue is for night, and metal stars like those on the vault are nailed throughout these areas. The white is for day, and lamps were hung there; today they are replaced with electric lights. Surrounding each light is a target-like series of concentric circles in black, white, yellow, and green. All this painting over the side aisles looks suspiciously fresh, and at its east end, on both sides, it covers Gothic ribbing which originally formed part of the transepts.

The façade of the church is a delightful carpenter-Gothic affair, with a trefolium over the door, pointed arches on each side, and much lattice-work; it is all painted white and has a pierced, embroidered look like a folk artist's drawing. The belfry is a little masterpiece. It is full of louvered ogival windows, steep little gables, and prim little pinnacles much like those painted on the lunettes inside. Only a disciple of Brother Michel, one suspects, would have thought of securing these pinnacles—or pretending to secure them—with flying buttresses.

To the right of the church is a little cemetery. Most of its graves are covered with slabs and upright markers of cement. Many are fenced in iron pipe, with crosses of the same material. Some have inscriptions in Chinese; others bear Hawaiian and Portuguese names. Red *ti* plants grow there, accenting the entire cemetery with their bursts of flame. The view to the west, down the slope to the coastal shelf and out to the Pacific, is one of the most magnificent on Hawaii. As one stands there in the rural silence, all the sounds of the atmosphere take on preternatural clarity—the chattering of the little boys playing in the open-air pavilion that serves the church as parish house, the sounds of the birds in the trees, and the eternal antiphony of crowing cocks from every point of the compass. This is a country church-yard which, somehow, inspires one to other thoughts than those of elegy.

Father Evarist Gielen who, as we have seen, studied painting with Father John in Belgium and is responsible for two other Painted Churches on the Island of Hawaii, was born in Vlytingen, Belgium, in 1897; was trained at the Sacred Hearts' Scholasticate in Father John's birthplace, Courtrai; and was ordained at Liége in 1925. After his ordination, he studied for a year at the Catholic University of America in Washington, D. C., and was then sent to the Hawaiian Islands, where he has remained. From 1927 to 1941 he served five Catholic parishes in the Puna district of the Big Island—those at Olaa, Kurtistown, Pahoa, Mountain View, and Kalapana. He built the Catholic churches which now stand in the last three of these five towns and painted the interiors of the last two. In later years he also painted pictures for the Catholic churches at Spreckelsville and Kahului on Maui, but the Spreckelsville pictures no longer exist.

The masterpiece of Father Evarist, who has been priest of the Church of the Sacred Hearts on Lanai since 1949, is his first effort, the church called

IX

27

Star of the Sea at Kalapana. This is as notable an achievement as Father John's Church at Honaunau, and it is difficult to understand why it has been totally ignored.

At Kalapana, as at Honaunau, one is deeply impressed with the totality of the structure, its telling relationship of painting and architecture, and the clarity of the entire concept. Like Father John, Father Evarist here emphasizes the three and the twice three in his windows, pictures, and other divisions of the building, although his plan is not so complex as the one at Honaunau.

The building is simply an oblong box with a large, barrel-vaulted ceiling and a recessed space, also barrel-vaulted, for the sanctuary at its east end. There is no division into nave and side aisles, and by contrast to Honaunau, where every visible inch inside the church is covered with decorative or figurative painting and there is no free wall space at all, the effect here is of a white interior in which the paintings are superbly placed. The openness of the space at Kalapana inspired Father Evarist to designs of heroic proportions; the pictures on the ceiling are approximately eight feet wide and ten feet tall, while the Nativity scene over the door reaches a width of twenty-two feet and is some fourteen feet high at its highest point.

Time has worked wonders with Father Evarist's color. His work could not have been very brilliant, high-keyed, or sharp in contrasts to begin with—he seems particularly to have liked a resonant gray—and with the cracking and flaking of the years his pictures have taken on an extraordinarily soft, delicate, woolly tone; they seem almost to be tapestries rather than paintings. Unfortunately, the windows below them are filled with garish-colored glass which at certain times of the day throws a very bad light. The visitor is urged to put his hand over the bridge of his nose in such a way as to exclude that light; when one does this, the color of the paintings cools down remarkably and their detail can be more carefully studied.

The Kalapana church has three windows in its left-hand wall and two windows and a confessional in the wall opposite. All the windows are double and take the traditional form of the tablets of the Ten Commandments; this form is echoed, somewhat larger, by the six paintings on the barrel-vaulted ceiling. The windows and the door of the confessional are framed with painted vine, leaf, and jewel motifs in gold and brown over blue, and this painting likewise finds an echo in the leafy adornment of the broad, black, wooden ribs which divide the ceiling into three large sections. Between each of the double windows stands a pair of Corinthian columns painted flat on the wall and seeming to support the thin moulding from which the barrel vault springs. Running the entire length of the wall is a

X. *Kalapana: General View of the interior*

red painted canopy from which hang five small scallops of drapery over each window and two large puffs behind the capital of each column.

Each of the three grand sections of the ceiling is subdivided by a pair of narrow painted ribs which start from their corners and proceed diagonally to cross at the apex of the barrel vault, leaving a large triangular area on each side; within these triangular areas appear the six large pictures previously mentioned. There is also a pictorial composition on the arch over the recess of the sanctuary and another on the ceiling of the sanctuary itself; and, as we have indicated, there is a huge Nativity on the lunette over the door at the west end.

Father Evarist tells us that in painting all these things his sole concern was to interest and instruct his parishioners and that he had neither time nor desire to indulge in originality. Three of his pictures and most of his decorative angels are derived from a publication, now largely forgotten, called *Le catéchisme en images;* he also drew upon two old masters, two nineteenth-century academicians, and one artist about whom we know nothing but who seems, to judge by internal evidence, also to belong in the nineteenth-century academic category. Very little in the church is Father Evarist's own and yet everything in it is his own; he has utterly transformed every motif he has touched and in most cases he has enormously heightened its pictorial value. He, and the processes of time which have given luster to his color, have made valid art out of the most commonplace hack work, such as that which appears in *Le catéchisme en images.*

This publication exists, or did exist, in two forms, both issued by La Maison de la Bonne Presse in Paris. Its first version, the date of which is uncertain, was a portfolio of sixty-eight large chromolithographs. Its second version was a book wherein the same pictures were reproduced as black-and-white engravings. The book appeared in French in 1908 and was reprinted, with its text translated into numerous different languages, in the immediately subsequent years: according to its foreword, this volume was brought out in order to place the pictures in the hands of those who could not afford the chromos. Father Evarist seems to have drawn upon both versions. He no longer possesses either, but we had the good fortune to discover an incomplete set of the color plates, and a copy of the book in its English edition of 1912, in the convent of the Helpers of the Holy Souls in San Francisco, and thanks to Mother Mary Loyola of that convent we are able to reproduce some of them.

The pictures are unsigned. The preface to the book asserts that "the most competent artists were employed" in making them, but their names are not given. Except insofar as they—or some of them—give off that faint whiff of watered-down Raphael so common to commercial religious illustration, these pictures do not appear to be indebted to the old masters or to anyone else. They have reached the embarrassing age of limbo through which all commercial art must pass before it is reborn as the quaint popular art of a remote period. They are not old enough to be interesting but they are too old to be useful. Catholic schools in general no longer employ them; the Bonne Presse has supplanted them with a new edition in modern style, and the old edition is preserved here and there, as at the convent of the Helpers of the Holy Souls, for such historic value as it may possess. But Father Evarist's touch has conferred the highest degree of vitality and spirit upon these lifeless, otherwise long-forgotten things.

In proceeding around the church at Kalapana, we shall discuss each painting as it appears today and contrast it, when possible, with the picture from which it comes. **X**

All the pictures on the ceiling were painted on a light blue ground, which shows through the crackle and flake and has much to do with their generally cool tone. Starting at the right near the door, these pictures are:

"The Death of Ahab." The wounded Ahab is being driven from the battlefield in his chariot, while the dogs lick up his blood. The two plunging horses are extremely high-spirited in their drawing and very nicely foreshortened. The whole painting today produces an effect of almost Whistlerian gray, and the figures of the soldiers at the left have been misted out, but the three figures in the chariot—Ahab, the charioteer, and an attendant who supports the wounded old man—retain something of the original richness of their color. The medallion above displays crossed keys and a crucifix.

This painting is an almost literal copy of Plate 42 in *Le catéchisme en images*. The original contained a group of soldiers in the right background as well as the left, but Father Evarist omitted most of these; and, as we have observed, nearly all the soldiers on both sides have disappeared with time. Father Evarist's color in the central group, and in the chariot and the horses, is darker and more resonant than that of the chromo, but the color composition in both versions is identical, and perhaps it is time that has transposed the Kalapana version to a lower key.

At this point an interpolation is in order.

At some time in the recent past, someone—nobody knows who—started to restore the faces, hands, and other exposed flesh parts in all the pictures at Kalapana but did not finish the job. He first painted the areas he desired to restore with flat white. Over this he drew eyes, noses, and other features 31 in black line. Last of all he added modeling in brownish flesh tones. The restorer, whoever he was, had the soul of an artist, and we may be thankful to him; he worked on all six of the paintings on the ceiling at Kalapana and on the Nativity in the lunette over the door, and in every case but two the pictures are much better for his assistance. He modeled Ahab's neck in brownish flesh tones but left his face flat white, with the features drawn in black outline. This passage reveals the three stages of the restorer's method.

Next after "The Death of Ahab" is a "St. Cecilia" derived from an unknown source. Father Evarist has forgotten his model here, and we have not been able to locate it. We thought for a time that the picture had been taken from the famous "St. Cecilia" of Carlo Dolci, but we were proven incorrect in this assumption by a curious, disturbing find: in the parish church of Acapulco, Mexico, one may see the very same "St. Cecilia"— a large, heavy, baroque lady with red hair who sits playing an organ to the delight of two *putti*, one of whom descends with the mincing gait of a tight-rope walker along the edge of a red drape thrown from the top of the organ. The only difference between the two versions is in their materials; the one in Acapulco is on canvas and rests in a lyre-shaped frame adorned with electric light sockets. Church authorities in Acapulco state that their picture has been in the church for many years and that its authorship is unknown. Both versions are probably copied from the same printed original—an original, in all likelihood, so widely scattered, not to say familiar and obvious, as to defy research. The medallion above the "St. Cecilia" at Kalapana contains the Lamb of God.

When the restorer reached "St. Cecilia," he dabbled some white paint on her chest, forehead, nose, and chin, and then stopped. Perhaps he realized that to restore St. Cecilia's very large areas of flesh tone would throw every-thing off balance, and not only in this particular picture but in the entire ceiling. At all events, St. Cecilia's unrestored hands, and the unrestored portions of her face and neck, give one a good idea of what the flesh parts of all the pictures looked like before the rehabilitation was attempted.

The last picture on the right-hand side is "The Mocking of Christ." Christ sits at the left in a red robe, surrounded by jeering figures which are remarkable for the brutality of their expressions. At the lower left a man sits drinking greedily from a bottle. The face of Christ, his right arm, and the face of the thug who stands behind him all bear traces of the unfinished restoration. In the medallion above is a monstrance surrounded by clouds.

According to Father Evarist, this painting was derived from one Ruys-broeck. The only Ruysbroeck we find recorded in any of the standard dictionaries of artists was a sixteenth-century architect, and he could not have been responsible for this "Mocking of Christ." The books contain entries for numerous painters with similar names—Reesbroeck, Rysbroeck, Rysbraeck, and so on—but they are all old masters, most of them were specialists in still life, and none of them fits. We are convinced, for reasons to be given later, that Father Evarist's Ruysbroeck was a fairly recent artist.

Starting at the door on the left-hand side of the church, the pictures appear in the following order:

"The Death of a Sinner." This title is inscribed on a ribbon within the painting itself. A sinner in a gray cloak is falling through space into the hands of red devils with green wings, surrounded by the flames of hell. Directly above the sinner is the inscribed ribbon, held by a fiend who is a particularly impish and delectable example of his breed. An angel in gray flies away from the sinner toward Christ and the cross at the extreme upper left. At the lower left, a sturdy, gray-haired pastor—clearly a portrait of St. John Vianney, the patron saint of parish priests—stands on a platform holding out his cross in a gesture of exorcism. Above the painting is a medallion showing a church on a rock.

This picture comes from Plate 56 of *Le catéchisme en images*, which is divided into two parts; it exemplifies the death of a just man in its upper half and the death of a sinner in its lower. The sinner's death is being witnessed by five members of his family, who occupy the lower left-hand corner, immediately under Christ and the cross in heaven. Father Evarist has omitted this family group and has placed the figure of the pastor directly below Christ and the cross; and it is Father Evarist who has given this priest the features of St. John Vianney. Father Evarist's powerful ripples, rhythms, and counter-rhythms cannot be found in the original. They arise in part from the fact that his figures are much flatter than those of the anonymous French artist; and his figures fill their space with a grandly scaled thrust and counterthrust of large, monumental forms completely foreign to the more detailed, crowded, and illustrational concept of the original.

In the *Catéchisme* version the sinner is not falling through a void into the hands of the demons; they are pulling him out of bed. Returning to the version at Kalapana, one sees that Father Evarist faithfully followed his model here, but time has effaced nearly all the evidences of the bed except the two square posts of its footboard and has thereby greatly enhanced the drama of the sinner's descent into hell. We originally "read" the posts of the footboard as two symbolic church towers separating the priest from the devils, and we regret the necessity of giving up that interpretation.

The *Catéchisme's* sinner is nude to his waist, and so was Father Evarist's sinner when the picture was fresh. The restorer has carried through his 33 restoration to completion only on "The Death of a Sinner," but he did not touch the sinner's torso and arms; here he restored only the hands, face, and neck, giving the figure a definite neckline and thereby transforming the unrestored gray of the torso and arms into a shirt. One suspects that he did this for æsthetic reasons. To have restored the torso and arms as well as the head, neck, and hands would have created a disturbingly large area of new paint and destroyed the effect of the picture. As it is, the entire surface of the painting is scattered with small accents of fresh white in the faces and hands of its *dramatis personæ*, and these add much to its pictorial and dramatic values.

Next after "The Death of a Sinner" is a painting we may call "The Guardian Angel." Two small children gather flowers in the woods by a lake, while the guardian angel stands over them, her hands outstretched to catch them if they should fall. The angel is a figure of extraordinary dignity and impressiveness, with heroic wings, black garments, and a rose-gray robe that defines the figure in a large, slow, baroque swirl. Time has worked magic with Father Evarist's woodland, transforming it into a misty-moist impressionistic garden, and giving the whole an extremely subtle and harmonious tone. The medallion above this painting contains a pelican.

"The Guardian Angel" is based upon a painting by the German artist, Bernhard Plockhorst (1825–1907), an engraving of which we found in Horne and Bewer's *The Bible and Its Story*. Father Evarist has reversed Plockhorst's composition, redeemed his angel and his children from their saccharinity, and heightened the appeal of the child figures by reducing their scale in relationship to the angel.

The third picture on the left-hand side is "Christ the King." The figure of Christ, elongated, statuesque, slightly Buddha-like, and greatly heightened in power through the white retouching of hands, face, and exposed foot, stands on a dais adorned along its edge with tiles; these are alternately black and red and are ornamented with geometric figures in gold. Christ wears a gray robe, a portion of which is thrown back about his body and over his left shoulder; this portion of the robe is modeled with rose-color and edged with floral and diamond-shaped motifs. In his left hand he holds an orb on which the map of Europe can be seen, and in his right hand he holds a scepter, very delicately balanced. He wears a jeweled crown, and behind his head is a gray halo enclosing a greenish-gold cross. At either side of the figure is a red column on a black base; the tops of these columns are obscured by puffs of drapery. Christ's throne is composed of a red-and-gold canopy and a red seat joined by an embroidery of black squares of two different sizes creating an abstract rhythm over a gray ground; this embroidery is edged in brown and gold. A blue drape serves as background for the entire painting. Its creator must have been especially proud of this majestic work, for it is the only picture in all the Painted Churches of Hawaii to display a signature; at the lower right one may read the inscription, "November 6 / 1930 / Evarist." In the medallion above are the Sacred Hearts of Jesus and Mary and the Crown of Thorns.

Father Evarist tells us that "Christ the King" was taken from a reproduction of a painting by Joseph Janssens (1854-1930), the same Joseph Janssens who so greatly impressed Father John in the post-Hawaiian phase of his career. Father Evarist no longer possesses this reproduction and we have been unable to locate a copy of it. We therefore cannot say with certainty that Father Evarist has ennobled Janssens as he ennobled Plockhorst and the unknown illustrators of *Le catéchisme en images;* it is worthy of note, however, that in the article on this artist in their *Allgemeines Lexikon der Bildenden Künstler*, Thieme and Becker credit him with little more than "an idealizing, often quite insipid conception of Biblical subjects."

On the arch over the recess containing the altar are four very lively angels bearing a ribbon inscribed "*Maria ka koku O ke kai e pale oe makou.*" **XI** This is translated into English along the lower edge of the arch: "Star of the Sea, pray for us." At the apex of the arch stands Mary holding the infant Jesus, clearly copied from Raphael's *Sistine Madonna*. A large gold star appears behind this figure, and behind that is blue sea. The sea and the Madonna's blue skirt have been restored. The skirt is now completely flat and merges with the sea behind it. Father Evarist's blues seem to have been particularly vulnerable to time, heat, and salt air, and the portions restored were probably in very bad condition indeed.

Father Evarist informs us that the wall behind the altar originally bore a painting representing the interior of a cathedral, but it is no longer there. The source of this idea is clear enough; what is not clear is how effective Father Evarist's cathedral could have been in so small a space.

The barrel-vaulted ceiling over the altar is painted with crossed ribs and graceful leaf forms like those used elsewhere in the church, and in its free spaces appear four angels whose large wings, flowing drapery, and extended gestures are the very essence of wind-whipped flight. All these angels look— with special appropriateness in a church named Star of the Sea—like the figureheads carved for ships by the master craftsmen of Salem in the days when New England whalers called at the Sandwich Islands. Three of them are exactly the same in posture, with one arm raised and the other placed   35 across the body. The fourth angel gestures downward, carrying a palm branch, and the outline of its body is curiously squared off. This angel is blue and is therefore badly flaked. The others are painted in green, brown, red, and gold and look almost fresh, but they have probably not been restored.

Two of the angels surrounding the Sistine Madonna on the arch are derived from those on the title page of *Le catéchisme en images* as issued in book form. The three relatively fresh-looking angels on the ceiling over the altar come from the same source, but the badly flaked blue one comes from the *Catéchisme*'s Plate 40, wherein it flies through the sky bearing a martyr's palm to St. Stephen, who is being stoned to death below.

In comparing the angels over the altar with their sources, one may see more dramatically than anywhere else in the church how signally the folk artist has improved on his model. In fitting these angels into a pre-established, geometrically outlined space, Father Evarist was forced to elongate their figures and place them horizontally rather than vertically; he simplified and enhanced the rhythm of their drapery, flattened the modeling of the figures, and in all but the blue angel reversed the curves of the wings, thereby enormously increasing the strength of each silhouette. He also gave these angels small heads with pointed chins and long, Modigliani-like noses; this is the final touch of departure from the anthropomorphic realism of his model.

The "Nativity" in the lunette over the door is the largest single picture in any of the Painted Churches; as we have seen, it is twenty-two feet wide and fourteen feet high at its highest point. In the center, an adoring Mary and Joseph kneel at either side of the Christ Child in his manger, while the ox and ass look on. In the sky, three gray angels with red hair display a ribbon inscribed "Glory to God on High." At the left a road winds off toward a castle from cavelike openings among the rocks. The entire right-hand side of this painting has been totally ruined and is now an illegible jumble of more or less geometric forms; originally this passage contained the figures of shepherds with their sheep.

The color in this painting is totally different from that to be seen elsewhere in the church. The red, blue, and gold of Mary's clothing and the rich brown and green of Joseph's robe have a distinctly Italianate flavor; there is also something Florentine about the "feel" of the drawing, and the road winding off among the rocks is a Florentine device. In fact, when we first became acquainted with this picture, we were convinced that, despite its use of such Northern motifs as Mary's wimple and the four-legged manger standing well off the ground, its ultimate source would be found in the vicinity of Botticelli, Filippino Lippi, or some other Florentine of their period. We were totally wrong, however. The source of the picture is Plate 2 bis of *Le catéchisme en images*. It is Father Evarist who was responsible for the Florentine atmosphere of his own version. He achieved this through beauty of color and the all but constant use of dark contour lines in place of the tonal modeling of the original; the subject does the rest. Only the central group and the angels above it came from the *Catéchisme*. The rocks and the road at the left and the now illegible shepherds at the right are Father Evarist's own. The face of his Madonna, like the faces of his angels over the altar, reminds one much of Modigliani. The face of the Christ Child has been restored with flat white and pops out of the composition. Here, as in "St. Cecilia," but only in these two pictures, the restorer's effort has had unfortunate results.

All the churches with which we are concerned contain painted plaster statues of the same period and style as the illustrations in *Le catéchisme en images*. They have a certain sweet charm, but they have no real sculptural quality; at Kalapana, however, there is some sculpture of more than ordinary interest. Although the large crucifix over the altar is also painted plaster, it was taken from a good model, and one can easily transfer it in imagination to some first-rate German wood-carver; and whoever placed that crucifix against a red drape had a genuine artist's instinct. The sanctuary rail is adorned with two fetching plaster angels, obviously Victorian; they seem originally to have been bronzed, but they have been painted over with white, leaving curious patches of the original bronze coating to show through. The candelabra they hold have acquired a magnificent patina with the years. On a blind window outside the church is a finely proportioned crucifix apparently made of aluminum. This seems an improbable material for a religious image; perhaps the crucifix has merely been covered with aluminum paint. All this sculpture appears to have been added after Father Evarist's time.

Father Evarist built St. Theresa's church in Mountain View in 1936, six **XII** years after he had completed his work at Kalapana. St. Theresa's is a distinctly less successful effort, for two reasons.

The first reason is that the painting was not done according to any organized plan. It was a money-raising project. Father Evarist asked the members of his congregation to subscribe for pictures, and the more the better: consequently the Mountain View church contains three paintings on its left-hand wall and six on its right, three paintings and a decorative panel of false windows on its barrel-vaulted ceiling over the nave, eighteen small paintings on the flat ceilings over the side aisles, a large Nativity scene behind the altar, six painted but empty niches around that altar, and, above the door, one more picture and several empty spaces for which, apparently, no subscribers could be found. The thing got out of hand, and the sense of relationship between the paintings, and between the paintings and the architecture, which is so strong and so important at Honaunau and Kalapana, is not to be found here at all.

The second reason for the less successful effect at Mountain View is that the pictures, except for those on the ceiling, were not painted *in situ* but were done on pieces of plyboard, at Father Evarist's rectory in Pahoa, and were put in place after they were finished. Protected from the back by an extra thickness of wood, they have not suffered from heat, and the atmosphere at Mountain View, at some little distance from the seacoast, apparently attacks pigment less severely than the atmosphere at Kalapana or Honaunau. Therefore, these pictures have not weathered, but by the same token, nothing has happened to mellow them. The processes of nature which have so greatly improved Father Evarist's work at Kalapana have not come to his aid here, and his colors retain their original garishness.

Father Evarist tells us that most of the pictures at Mountain View are adapted from the mysterious Ruysbroeck. Many of their figures are in an elongated, drawn-out, Aubrey Beardsleyan style which seems to place Ruysbroeck in the 1890's. Ruysbroeck may also be responsible for the church's profusion of spiraling baroque forms; swirls of smoke on altars and waves breaking stormily are everywhere to be seen. Many of these passages are quite effectively done, but they also contribute to the hectic, disorganized feeling of the church as a whole. Perhaps its most effective single panel is one of the three on the ceiling, wherein a one-legged, Michelangelesque God the Father divides the light of day from the darkness of night.

XIII We have reserved until the end discussion of a church which few will ever see because it is a deserted ruin in an inaccessible place. No road leads to Maria Lanakila (Mary of Victory), near the shore at Kealia, close to Honaunau, and it can be approached only by a jouncing jeep ride along the beach. It is said to have been built in 1860, long before Father John came to Hawaii, but tradition credits him with its interior painting, and in this case tradition is probably correct; the work here has many traits in common with that at Honaunau.

Since the earthquake of 1950, which destroyed the building, population along this part of the Kona Coast has largely moved away from the shore-side villages to those on the higher ground along the road about two miles away. Consequently, no effort has been made to rebuild Maria Lanakila; it has been abandoned to the wasps and ferns, its wooden roof has fallen in to form a crazy heap of rotten boards inside its walls of plastered lava rock, and its belfry and steeple lie upended on the ground like some huge animal grotesque in death. Still, much remains here, and it is possible to arrive at a fairly accurate picture of what the church was like in its heyday. It was the smallest of the Painted Churches—inside it was scarcely more than thirty feet long and twenty feet wide—and everything in it was done in diminutive proportions; it must have been the most vivacious and delicately tasteful church of them all.

Its entire color scheme was keyed to a single, simple, and very effective contrast—that between the white of the walls and the reddish brown of the painted dado, about three feet high, which still runs around three sides of the interior and is repeated, in a much narrower band, around the top of the walls outside, at the point where the wooden roof joined on.

The ceiling was barrel-vaulted over the central aisle and flat over the side aisles; it was entirely covered with light blue paint and was spangled with stars in the same reddish brown as the dado. The vault was supported on square columns, also in red-brown, adorned with painted white ribbons, shorter than those at Honaunau, angularly stylized, and bearing no inscriptions. There were two of these columns on either side of the central aisle and there were two pairs of false columns—flat boards set against the east and west walls—painted in the same fashion as the free-standing ones. All bore capitals, like those at Honaunau, made of prefabricated moulding and nailed on about five inches from the top.

On either side of the altar stood a tiny sacristy, partitioned off with wood. The partitions were painted white and covered with innumerable rosettes, light gray in tone, and sketchily dabbled on; their effect today is like that of a palely figured wallpaper. Between the two sacristies stood an altar which might well have been a French interior decorator's special pride and delight. It has long since fallen apart—we have removed such fragments of it as remain in order to preserve them—and so there is no point in describing it in detail. Suffice it to say that it rejoiced in orange and white, that its most remarkable feature was a pair of baskets filled with flowers painted on its backboard, to the right and left of the tabernacle, in a sketchy effervescent, impressionistic and altogether enchanting style, and that it harmonized to perfection with the rather strange and wonderful painting that stood on the wall above and behind it.

This painting, done directly on the plaster, is still there, or, to put it more accurately, part of it is there. It has stood for a decade directly exposed 39 to the Hawaiian sun and rain. It is deeply fissured and large areas of it have crumbled away. It looks more like a relic of the first century than of the early twentieth, partly because of its condition and partly because of its style.

It is all painted on a ground tone of the same reddish brown as the dado, the columns, and the stars. Its composition is horizontal, and photographs of it taken some years ago, before the destruction had proceeded as far as it has gone today, show that it was originally divided into two equal areas by a cross of the same bright orange as was used in the altar beneath it. A young girl dressed in white, her face and arms reddish brown, kneels at the cross on the left-hand side. To the right of the cross stands a handsomely voluminous figure of Mary, in a blue robe and a white wimple, with white drapery over the upper part of her figure, gesturing toward the kneeling girl. Behind Mary stands Jesus, his face a deep brown, his robe bright orange. The brown ground-tone shows through all the figures and serves as a general background as well. Mary's face is in profile and bears a strong resemblance to that of the seated figure with hands clasped on the table which appears immediately below Daniel in "The Handwriting on the Wall" at Honaunau; here, too, and even more strikingly than at Honaunau, the eye is seen frontally despite the profile view.

It is clear, then, that Kealia and Honaunau share many features, both of structure and of painting. Since Kealia is the older building, and its general style is simpler, we suggest that Father John's work there was done before he built the church at Honaunau and that Honaunau represents an effort to accomplish something on a more elaborate and ambitious scale. At Honaunau Father John had daring. At Kealia he had, in the finest sense of the word, chic.

XIV

No tour parties go, or ever will go, to Kealia. Honaunau is their favorite point of pilgrimage, and the tour guides tell many a fine tale about this church, or, rather, about its creator—how Father John spent fifteen years painting the pictures by candlelight, how he translated the Bible into Hawaiian, how he returned to Belgium at the outbreak of the first world war and was killed in a German air raid. We trust that the publication of this book will not put an end to these stories. A church like St. Benedict's of Honaunau breeds legends, and folklore has its place by the side of truth.

As one sits in a pew at St. Benedict's, surrounded by its paintings, which seem to be so much older than they really are, one's mind goes back to a gorgeously cadenced line in an older version of the language which Father John invariably used for his entries in the baptismal book:

XI. *Kealia: Fragment, Madonna*

Au moustier voy dont je suis paroissienne
Paradis paint, ou sont harpes et lus....

Or to quote the final stanza of Villon's ballade in the magnificent prose paraphrase of John Millington Synge:

I'm a poor aged woman was never at school and is no scholar with letters, but I've seen pictures in the chapel with Paradise on one side, and harps and pipes in it, and the place on the other side, where sinners do be boiled in torment; the one gave me great joy, the other a great fright and scaring; let me have the good place, Mother of God, and it's in your faith I'll live always.

Fifteenth-century Paris finds an echo here on the Island of Hawaii. St. Benedict's is a little corner of medieval Europe among the coffee trees.

There were great painters in Courtrai, Louvain, Bruges, Ghent, and other small towns of Belgium in François Villon's time. Father John was not their equal in craftsmanship but he was a descendant of their spirit. If, by some miracle, a Jan van Eyck or a Rogier van der Weyden could see the paintings at Honaunau, one suspects he would smile and understand.

41

P. 4. CONGREGATION OF THE SACRED HEARTS: The complete, official name of this order is Congregation of the Sacred Hearts of Jesus and Mary and of the Perpetual Adoration of the Most Holy Sacrament of the Altar. In Europe it is often called the Congregation of Picpus, after the name of the street in Paris on which its first Mother House is located.

P. 5. ROBERT LOUIS STEVENSON: *In the South Seas* (New York, 1891), Chapter VII.

P. 5. MICHEL BLANC: Information from Bishop Louis Tirilly, Vicar Apostolic to the Marquesas, and from the archives of the Congregation of the Sacred Hearts in Rome.

P. 6. FATHER JOHN'S ARTICLES: A complete list of these will be found in Robert Streit, *Bibliotheca Missionum*, Vol. XXI (Freiburg, 1955), p. 332. These articles are very well written, with no trace of naïveté about them. They are full of vivacious observation of people and places, and record Father John's triumphs and failures as an apostle to the Polynesians, but in all of them there is only one brief, ambiguous comment on painting: in recounting a visit which the Father Provincial of the Sacred Hearts made to South Kona in 1901, Father John says he made a permanent record of the day by painting a portrait of that dignitary on horseback, and he adds, "I had not done that kind of painting for some years." As we have pointed out in the main body of our text, Father John illustrated his articles with his own drawings, but whatever stylistic pecularities they may have exhibited were destroyed by the wood engravers who prepared all illustrations for publication in those days. Among the published drawings of Father John is a portrait of Vaekehu, the famous ex-cannibal "queen" of the Marquesas, whose strange story so deeply interested Stevenson. It may be found in *Les missions catholiques*, Vol. XXIII, p. 44. Copies of Father John's articles, and of all the other documents employed by the present authors, will be deposited with the Hawaiiana Department of the Gregg M. Sinclair Library, University of Hawaii.

P. 7. FATHER GÉRARD CHAULET: Quoted in Siméon Delmas, *Essai d'histoire de la mission des Iles Marquises* (Paris, 1929), p. 325.

P. 8. GAUGUIN: The only detailed, reliable account of Gauguin's life in the Marquesas is to be found in the article by Georges Le Bronnec, entitled *Les Dernières années*, published in the special Gauguin number of the *Gazette des beaux-arts* (98th year, 6th series, Vol. 47, dated 1956 but actually published in 1958), pp. 189-200. For an example of Gauguin's mingling of Breton and Polynesian folk motifs, see the drawing entitled "Les saints images" reproduced in *Paul Gauguin's Intimate Journals* (Bloomington, Indiana, 1958), p. 103.

P. 16. PAINTED APSE AND TRANSEPTS: The altar wall was first painted with false windows of the same shape and size as the real windows in the side walls. The cathedral apse was painted over them, but their outlines can still be seen in a raking light. We suspect that this tame adornment was not there long before it was covered with the masterpiece which is there now.

p. 16. NOTHING AT ALL DIRECTLY BEHIND THE ALTAR: It has been suggested that Father John did paint the area directly behind the altar but that this painting has flaked off and has therefore been covered over. We have not been able to remove the mat, but our interpretation of its being there is strongly supported by the fact that there is no painting, and never has been any, in the triangular space directly behind the projecting, steeply gabled roof of the altar. This unpainted space is slightly smaller than the present altar-roof and proves that an altar of the same general shape, but not quite so tall, stood in the church in Father John's time and was taken into consideration in planning the total design; the peak of its roof must have pointed to the face of Christ in the stained-glass window of the painted apse which the present altar slightly obscures. Although all the painting in the church has suffered extensive damage, there is no area in which the paint film has been totally destroyed. The greatest damage has occurred on the side walls, the exteriors of which are exposed to the sun. The altar wall, however, is shielded from the sun on its exterior side because of the sacristy which stands behind it.

p. 16. DAGUERRE: Information from Helmut and Alison Gernsheim, *L. J. M. Daguerre, the World's First Photographer* (Cleveland, 1956), *passim*. Quotation from Gernsheim, p. 121.

p. 19. MOTTOES OF ST. BENEDICT'S MEDAL IN HAWAIIAN: These inscriptions are as follows:

1. *O ke kea hemolele kou malamalama.* (The Holy Cross be my light.)

2. *Hele oe pela e Satana.* (Begone, Satan.)

3. *He poino kou mea i ninini mai ai.* (Literally, "You have poured forth trouble." The inscription on the medal reads, *Nunquam suade mihi vana*—"Do not suggest to me thy vanities.")

4. *Aole Satana kou alakai.* (Literally, "Satan is not your guide." The original is *Non draco sit mihi dux*—"Let not the dragon be my guide.")

5. *Ua oki oe me kou mea pau wale.* (Literally, "Stop with your perishable things." The original is *Sunt mala quae libas*—"Evil are the things thou profferest.")

6. *Nau no e inu kou poino.* ("Drink your own misfortune." The original is *Ipse venena libas*—"Drink your own poison.")

p. 26. FATHER EUGENE OEHMEN: Article in *Hilo Tribune*, Catholic Church Centennial Edition (Hilo, Hawaii, 1940), p. 4.

XII. *Father John Berchmans Velghe, SS.CC.*

XIII. *Father Evarist Gielen, SS.CC.*

PLATES

HONAUNAU

XV. *Honaunau: General view of the interior*

XVI. *North wall*

XVII. *South wall*

XVIII. *Palm tree on the vault*

XIX. *Vaulted ceiling over the nave*

XX. *Louis Daguerre: Painting behind altar in church at Bry-sur-Marne*

XXII. *Painted transept*

XXIII. *Painted transept*

XXIV. *Duccio di Buoninsegna: The Temptation of Christ*

XXV. *The Temptation of Jesus*

XXVI. *Detail, The Temptation of Jesus*

XXVII. *The Axenstrasse*

XXVIII. *The Appearance of the Cross to St. Francis*

XXIX. *Hell*

XXX. *Detail, Hell*

XXXI. *Detail, Symbolic of a Good Death*

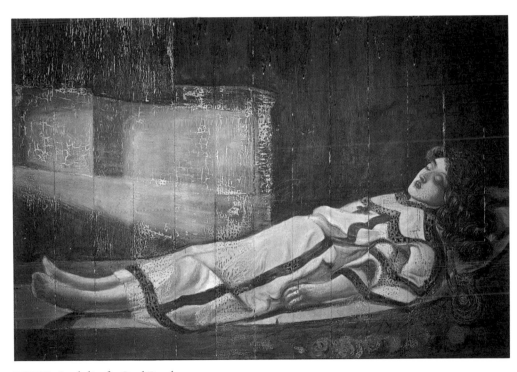

XXXII. *Symbolic of a Good Death*

XXXIII. *Karl Gebhardt: Eve Finding the Body of Abel*

XXXIV. *Cain and Abel* (*and Eve trying to revive him*)

XXXV. *Lunette*

(overleaf) XXXVI. *Detail of Lunette, Paul*
XXXVII. *Detail of Lunette, Peter*

KEALIA

XXXIX. *Domed interior*

XL. *Detail, Madonna*

KALAPANA

XLII. *Interior*

XLIII. Le catéchisme en images: *The Death of Ahab*

XLIV. *The Death of Ahab*

XLV. *Carlo Dolci: St. Cecilia*

XLVI. *St. Cecilia*

XLVII. *Detail, The Mocking of Christ*

XLVIII. *The Mocking of Christ*

XLIX. Le catéchisme en images: *The Death of a Sinner*

L. *The Death of a Sinner*

LI. *The Guardian Angel*

LII. *Christ the King*

LIII. *Detail, Christ the King*

LIV. Le catéchisme en images: *Angels*

LV. *Angels over the Altar*

LVI. *The Nativity* (overleaf)

LVII. *Detail, The Nativity*

LIST OF PLATES

PLATES

XII   Father John Berchmans Velghe, ss.cc. (*photograph courtesy of Mary Kalohi*)

XIII   Father Evarist Gielen, ss.cc. (*photograph courtesy of Francis Tongg*)

KALAPANA

I   Detail, Angels Over the Altar

X   General view of the interior

XLI   Exterior

XLII   Interior

XLIII   *Le catéchisme en images:* The Death of Ahab

XLIV   The Death of Ahab

XLV   Carlo Dolci: St. Cecilia

XLVI   St. Cecilia

XLVII   Detail, the Mocking of Christ

XLVIII The Mocking of Christ

XLIX   *Le catéchisme en images:* The Death of a Sinner

L   The Death of a Sinner

LI   The Guardian Angel

LII   Christ the King

LIII   Detail, Christ the King

LIV   *Le catéchisme en images:* Angels (taken from the border of the table of contents page)

LV   Angels over the Altar

LVI   The Nativity

LVII   Detail, The Nativity

MARQUESAS

II   Father John Berchmans Velghe: Portrait of Brother Michel Blanc (original in the archives of the Congregation of the Sacred Hearts, Rome)

III   Michel Blanc: Church at Taaoa, Hivaoe, Marquesas (*photograph by Fred Johnson*)

IV   Michel Blanc: Relief on the façade of the Church at Taaoa, Hivaoe, Marquesas (*photograph by Fred Johnson*)

V   Michel Blanc: Relief on the façade of the Church at Atuona, Hivaoe, Marquesas (*photograph by Fred Johnson*)

VI   Michel Blanc: Church at Atuona, Hivaoe, Marquesas (*photograph by Fred Johnson*)

VII   Michel Blanc: Angels Over the Altar, Church at Atuona

HONAUNAU

VIII   General view of the interior showing nave and side aisles

IX   The Handwriting on the Wall

XIV   Exterior

XV   General view of the interior

XVI   North wall

XVII   South wall

XVIII   Palm tree on the vault

XIX   Vaulted ceiling over the nave

XX   Louis Daguerre: Painting behind altar in church at Bry-sur-Marne, France (*photograph by Claude Calame*)

XXI   Burgos Cathedral, showing transept, cimborio, piers, etc.

XXII   Painted transept

XXIII   Painted transept

XXIV   Duccio di Buoninsegna: Temptation of Christ (*copyright the Frick Collection, New York*)

XXV   The Temptation of Jesus

XXVI   Detail, The Temptation of Jesus

XXVII   The Axenstrasse (from Oscar Kuhns: *Switzerland*, 1910)

XXVIII   The Appearance of the Cross to St. Francis

XXIX   Hell

XXX   Detail, Hell

XXXI   Detail, Symbolic of a Good Death

XXXII   Symbolic of a Good Death

XXXIII   Karl Gebhardt: Eve Finding the Body of Abel

XXXIV   Cain and Abel (and Eve trying to revive him)

XXXV   Lunette above The Appearance of the Cross to St. Francis

XXXVI   Detail of Lunette, Paul

XXXVII   Detail of Lunette, Peter

KEALIA

XI   Fragment, Madonna

XXXVIII   Kealia

XXXIX   Domed Interior

XL   Detail, Madonna

ACKNOWLEDGMENTS

This is not a big book, but it could not have been written without the help of numerous collaborators whose assistance we should like to acknowledge here.

We are indebted, first and foremost, to the Reverend Francis Kelliher, M.M., who, at the time our investigation was in progress, was priest of St. Benedict's Church, Honaunau, and was more a partner in our project than a contributor to it. The Reverend Evarist Gielen, ss. cc., of the Church of the Sacred Hearts, Lanai City, gave us much invaluable information. The Reverend Joseph McGinn, M.M., of Star of the Sea Church, Kalapana, and the Reverend James McLaughlin, M.M., of St. Theresa's Church, Mountain View, were also unfailingly kind and co-operative.

Our efforts would have been fruitless without the help of the Reverend Arsene Daenen, ss. cc., of the Sacred Hearts' Seminary, Hauula, who undertook research for us in Rome and in Belgium; the Very Reverend Brendan Furtado, ss. cc., Father Provincial of the Congregation of the Sacred Hearts in Hawaii, who opened his records to us; Mrs. Mary Kawena Pukui of the Bernice P. Bishop Museum, Honolulu, who acted as our Hawaiian translator, and Dr. Walter Heil and Mr. Vincent Stegman of the M. H. de Young Memorial Museum, San Francisco, who gave us the benefit of their experience in solving, or attempting to solve, problems of iconography which arose in connection with our studies of the paintings at Honaunau and Kalapana.

Our study of the work of Michel Blanc was brought to a successful conclusion because of the aid we were given by the Very Reverend Louis Tirilly, Vicar Apostolic to the Marquesas; Dr. Bengt Danielsson of Papeete, Tahiti; M. Georges Le Bronnec and M. Alfred Tissot of Atuona, Hivaoe; and Mr. Fred Johnson of Anapoo, Tahuata, who photographed the churches at Atuona and Taaoa at our request. Dr. Bradford Booth of the University of California both guided and commiserated with us through a long investigation which was well worth undertaking even though its results were entirely negative—our effort to find the photographs taken by Robert Louis Stevenson's stepson, Lloyd Osbourne, in the Marquesas in 1888. Mrs. Lilian Thomas, cultural officer of the French Consulate General in San Francisco, was extremely helpful to us in establishing contacts with many persons in French Polynesia.

The Reverend Patrick O'Reilly, s.m., of Paris, historian of the Catholic missions in the South Seas, and the Reverend Amerigo Cools, ss. cc., archivist of the Congregation of the Sacred Hearts in Rome, were immensely helpful to us in both the Marquesan and the Hawaiian phases of our research.

As always, the staffs of the Frick Art Reference Library and the New York Public Library were heroic in their efforts on our behalf.

The designer of so beautiful a volume as this ought to have his name on the title page as one of the authors. To acknowledge the collaboration of Mr. Kenneth Kingrey in a few words is to do him a rank injustice; but the book itself speaks for him. The enthusiasm and editorial wisdom displayed by Mrs. Aldyth V. Morris and Mr. Thomas Nickerson of the University of Hawaii Press were also major factors in bringing this project to a mature and successful conclusion. Finally, we should like to express our gratitude to Mr. Ralph Kiyosaki for assistance rendered us while the book was in production.

A. F.
N. C.

ANGELS OVER THE ALTAR *was printed at the Plantin Press, Los Angeles. The text is composed in Monotype Aldine Bembo, fourteen point, and the extracts, notes, and acknowledgments in twelve point, with display in various sizes of Bembo. The text has been printed by letterpress and the plates by offset on Curtis Colophon. The end leaves and coverings are handmade Nelson-Whitehead Roma Blue and Roma Sand. The binding was produced by the Earle Gray Bookbinding Company. The book was designed by Kenneth Kingrey and its production supervised by Aldyth Morris for the University of Hawaii Press, Honolulu.*